AIM STRAIGHT
AT THE FOUNTAIN
AND PRESS VAPORIZE

Elizabeth Marie Young

Cover image by   Matei Apostolescu

Book layout by   Colie Collen
Book design by   Fence Books

Published in the United States by   Fence Books
                                    Science Library 320
                                    University at Albany
                                    1400 Washington Avenue
                                    Albany, NY 12222
                                    www.fenceportal.org

Fence Books are distributed by   University Press of New England
                                    www.upne.com

and printed in Canada by   Westcan Printing Group
                                    www.westcanpg.com

Library of Congress Cataloguing in Publication Data
        Young, Elizabeth Marie [1975–]
        Aim Straight at the Fountain and Press Vaporize/ Elizabeth Marie
        Young

Library of Congress Control Number: 2009924812

ISBN 1-934200-24-7
ISBN 13: 978-1-934200-24-7

FIRST EDITION

FENCE BOOKS are published in partnership with the University at Albany
and the New York State Writers Institute, and with help from the New York
State Council on the Arts, the National Endowment for the Arts, and the
friends of *Fence*.

AIM STRAIGHT
AT THE FOUNTAIN
AND PRESS VAPORIZE

Elizabeth Marie Young
WINNER OF THE MOTHERWELL PRIZE

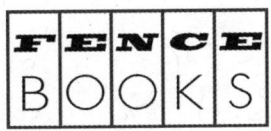

ALBANY, NEW YORK

Acknowledgments

Thank you to all the lovers of poetry at UC–Berkeley who created the community that gave rise to this book; to Rebecca Wolff, the best editor I could have asked for; and to those enthusiastic readers who helped me undertake, understand, and improve these poems: Dan Bouchard, Chris Daniels, Trane DeVore, Judith Goldman, Joel Nickels, Karla Nielsen, Ryan Murphy, and, especially, Margaret Ronda.

Many thanks to the editors of the following publications for publishing this work: *14 Hills, 26, New American Writing, Vanitas, Viz Inter-Arts Anthology,* ed. Roxi Power Hamilton, and *Word/for Word.*

Contents

Aim Straight at the Fountain and Press Vaporize

This is how innocence feels when lavender extract finagles
the bloodsucking tides into formulas pumped with pro-vitamin
B and the dirigibles (all joking aside) swell open like bloggers,
mid-sentence, and shrug off the urge to engulf all the clouds
in their high-minded cyclotron's mirth. So spare me the bit
about dead languages. This is not about love. It's about body-
wash flowing into the sea, daggers thrown in the dirt and the
plagiarists scrimming our grim penetralia's possible. Look in
the shatterless glass of the sun's orrery. We can read the spare
outl ne of birds flying north in our social security numbers and
mc h refrains of old songs like mechanical brides unplugged
lon enough to admire the sheets. They are white as Ophélia's
ubicomp angustifolia suckled on pluots and drowning in
monochrome blitz like a wunderkid high on the raw promises of
those huge sushi eyes.

Among the Seekers of Ether

Let's go get lost among the ether seekers squinting
in despair as people from the 18th century hang brightly in
the air dissecting bits of cloud (they're only waiting for a cue
from Newton to begin their vague descent). If you could take
the square root of this mass that we inhabit you would find a
fully fledged motet caught in the shadow of the memories the
centrifuge once ravaged as though honoring the dead with a
chilled and useless flourish. "It waxeth wet," she says, concealing
Vesta's fires in the folds of her new love (she has a passion for
Racine). But Crazy Jane just shrugs and love begins to melt
away. "Divide the air from air. Divide the castles from the
clouds. Divide the light from light, but if you dare sequester
my inertia in your tragedy I'll clasp the weary hand of god and
let him drag me in a straight line to the back of your cathedral
where pentangles are smashed to fit inside the roving spheres
the invalids ingest on their way back from the sea." Despite their
prayers, it wouldn't part. But if you listened very closely, you
could hear the feeble march revive inside their chests. They had
wanted to see flames but they could only see a single molecule, a
bit deranged and accidentally inspiring the smell of violets from
the surrounding air. And still they lurched and dragged their
rickety old model up the mountain where they leapt off into the
huge distance waving feathers pulled from caps that had dropped
below the treeline. Another great wave shook the night, moving
flagrantly through nothing, dulling bullets in their flight.

Another Ruler Thrones Triumphantly atop His House of Fame

The maharaja's mirror blindness left the harem worn
and listless. Tell me, sir, what will we do without our beautiful
Narcissus? We have come to see his face as pure reflection of the
health and beauty that surrounds us frail as glass. Of course we
all take pleasure playing fairies. Oberon assigns us roles swift as a
horse cavorting. But the prince is six years old! And now his eye
turns toward her breasts and soon his vanity will swell to colonize
the clouds she watches. Never mind the infidels. What we are
they wish to be. This mirror's blinder than a prism. Suddenly
the halls are filled with syllogisms. If our breaths traverse the
border, eyewitnesses will stray back through the pilasters and
tug upon the faded rope that is just hanging from the oval like a
cloak made out of flesh. Oh, ardent patch of sky! Such a bleary
gloss on death will not wring answers from the oracle or keep
our children clean. The winter of our lives engenders endless
cognates, pornographic monosyllables to rhyme with each new
baby's name. A few grotesques *en Italiano,* flamboyant in the
hope that one day all the wooden wands will snap and they'll
be free to watch the hunchback ring his bells. Then again, *bad*
history only constructs its hall of mirrors out of happy endings.
"Throned in state, the ample body…"

Master, lead us back to Rome. We want a city so abstract
and tinged with pink, it will try to nestle in the petals of your
single dreaming eye.

As the Evening Primrose Crimps the Skyline's Opulent Toilette

"How humbling, the wastefulness of winter in Dubai. Better than a newborn star or a symphony in white noise shrill as ice caps cracking on a transatlantic flight, a sound serene as Botticellis watching life just pass them by."

The other narcissists whip out their samovars and drink to post-traumatic stress, their elusive edges bleeding through the neighbor's chainlink fence (a no-man's land by candlelight, listless and fungible as nametags peeled off silhouettes). "Confusion to mathematics!" How lucky we are to be but suicidal flirts in a texture so far-reaching it drowns the hovercraft in its own pretentious thrill strung out on crystal meth and delicate beading. Bemoan your lost vacation days, high-voltage quadrupeds! Adjust your rosy goggles, this is not just any lightning. Finger the circumflex wound round your ancestors' gills as they reached for the unfathomable heights of a high E— Quadruple sowtow, party on! Aurora throws up sprays of atoms. Her quotidian is rife with shaggy prodigies streaming through the underbrush to the Wondrous Rhineheart Chill. Poised beneath triumphal arcs, operatically and so on.

As Rock Strata Shift Infinities Pause Like Ancient Words Chipped Off Marble Facades

It's sad when your theories turn out to be flawed. The factory girls think they've found god in the cheery *ciao bella*s the sailors unfurl like doves at their feet. Nightingales fondle the rotary phones. But the mountains don't mind. They are poised to touch stars in large print for the blind. Now the eagle has landed. The blazon has flecked each wrist with its swerve and the erstwhile's caress urges us toward the beauty of reckless abstractions: Technocrats fed to the beast, ego trips and gamma rays sunk to the earth's very core. Those girls have seen god but they want more than a dirty blond dragged through the wake of real time, more than fly-by-night quarks and the endless wet dreams of a State scientist. They want joy! They want peace! The genome unravels and everything fixates on unexplained crime and malingers, agog: Is the earth really dying? Will innocence claw its way to the heart of the earth where the sound of our footsteps is silent as falling asleep, revealing our past lives like statues collecting invisible factoids the fact-checkers missed?

Ballad of a Disembodied Escapologist

No, *you* stock up on no-fuss smart foods, rodent genius.
Twiggy, shoo, you're not my inner interlocutor.
       It's right there for the asking: a seven-headed dragon
masterwork on microfiche. The "I don't care" girl mellowing away
in silent déjà vu. Kundalini prodigies, enough gobstopping let's
be honest—you're not really double-jointed. Hold your breath,
the sky turns blue and then the strobe light splits your tango
into sluttish memories of a sine-wave's landlocked sinecure. I'm
sore and tired of multitasking. *Yes,* we need junk hauled away.
But silken threads instead of tongues are wonders you once said
would be the death of any kisser. And the feeling made us bold.
But then electrostatic whispers peeled the paint straight off the
walls and singed the master shadowlist.
                    Of course the world needs interlarding
with a brainchild's hit and run. Just watch them lick their finger
bowls. But would you do that to your mother? Like wearing gold
lamé in Vegas with Chernobyl left on pause. You're, like, *yelling* at
me and I bought all these sportsbras.

But Now That Too Is Gone So I Will Drink Until I'm Dead

I've slept with all the village girls. They kept me company while I was droning and the fissures of their stony alchemies held promises of healing sharp and swift as childbirth. They used to ask, "My little pigeon, why so sick?" then they would burn like gravel in my hands. Not quite earth-shattering and yet so stark and full of lust I couldn't answer. So I'd toss out ironies of glass. I'd drag their family trees across the Caucuses. The battered branches tore my hands perhaps suggesting human consciousness, or nothingness. Please understand, I loved each separate syllable of each girl's separate name. Scrubbing soil from their faces, thinking rarely of the land or the corrugated anthems they had written when the wires weren't yet crossed. Dragana, I have come to save you but you're sick of being saved. And now my diary is full of lead. Let's prick it back to life and watch the sky purr overhead.

Counting Pebbles While the Sibyl Shrivels
in Her Jar

It's unruly come mid-summer. Lovebirds quiver and
ignite astride our grimly thinning shadows. The light rain
is replete with the smell of belly-dancing and the sound of
fingertips alive as tessellating birds in search of a peckable feast.

How beastly (we infer) just marginalia and strings
reverberating to the frolic of some daydream-weaver's frond.
Reduced to joystick jubilation. Tenderness the pink of things not
really even born. How colorful! I can't go on like this outraged by
every glint of the brandy drinker's eye, swooning at the limberlost
and waiting for a throng of loved ones to march in, pull the IV
out and feed me to the sound of one hand clapping.

Don't look now, our summer bride has entered the
gazebo thinking this might be a film noir ready to unwind.
Swaying like a wan Noguchi, she cuts the sky in half and as bells
begin to peel screams out "diaphanous!" Look how the rainbows,
mesmerized, bow euphemistic heads drinking deeply of dresses
never to be worn again. But the bridesmaids just keep talking.
And children, though unborn, refuse to turn the other cheek.
Meanwhile, fresh-cut orchids are too opulent to speak.

April's cruel—that's not a joke. The bodies scattered so
pell-mell you can't just leave the rest to science or squeegee
up the pain. You try to check it for a pulse, hidden cameras go
"ping" and you're left heaving in the silence of some momentary
waxwing.

Daughters of Anubis You Think You Have All the Answers

You scan so seamlessly into the strained pentameter of this crude forest—but the trees are dying in hexameters. They've blasted the angel of death into glass figurines that smash at your feet. Soon they will squeeze stones for blood. Another miracle. So eat your heart out Cleopatra. Stick your milkwhite fist into your giant mouth and gloat. Don't let a little mist rising from the river fool you into thinking you can eat your baby oysters raw. Remember Antony? The earth will never seem so round as it was that graceless night you wandered through the Grand Bazaar while students in their robes talked god and politics among the imitation pearls. It's now time to bring another little Ceasar into this world as it sinks back into sand (of course, Nijinsky was enthralled and left a phantom limb outstretched above the ditch where they had tossed their chaperones). But my dear princess, you are numb and naked. Never mind, you're still alive and your pierced tongue can savor the taste of a victory you never knew—a much bigger pearl than even Pompey used for eyes. You see, another world awaits you just beyond this field of columns where your bones rust back into the earth like tattoos of lost poems written by some prima donna before the world grew wary of the eunuchs geeking out. They're so Baryshnikov, it's scary.

Don't Get Me Started, Pink Eye, It's Just Part of the Decor

Who are these mercenary spirits? They have come to lead the dead into the glass conservatory where an existential rain still glimmers on the beveled edges of our human thoughts. Don't touch, just watch them blink to life and feel your fingers disappearing even as you point (the young were making goulish faces at the carnivores who fled to higher elevations to hide their dreary spots among the decomposing plastic bags that hung in molten canopies). Perhaps the prophets had been wrong about the future but the past was still unfolding from beyond their atmospheric plans. They had clung for many years to the edge of that forever, doing back flips off a dock and breathing all the air as if it were hashish leaked from the open mouths of restless, roving beasts who lived inside the park. They were willing to believe that, from the bare rooms in the upper regions, they could see the sea. But as they sat there, getting older in the dungeon of their lie they sometimes found themselves forgetting. Oh, how your cities rise, their secrets cradled in the bedrock until the day they streak across the dunes toward an oasis. In the meantime, there is dawn, and the panther stretched in anguish across your new divan.

Dr. Izmesteva Has Now Analyzed the Data

Now that Dr. Izmesteva has analyzed the data, we can
be sure Scheherazade would sooner bite her tongue than let
the sleeping beauty dream about her reading Proust or was it
Joyce, I can't remember. The earthquakes have begun to clamor
for attention. But the scientists have strayed off to the Magic
Mountain where the public will obey them blindly as a yogi
turning softly on his head. The numbers don't add up. I think the
thousandth night has bled back through the rising terror like a
specter of the wave our princess holds between her teeth. What
if the earth cracks open, saving us from having to learn French?
What if the sorrows that we feel at night while in the nursery
are nothing? Then you'd smile more politely *ma chérie.* Perhaps
you'd even lapse into an ice age once again and reject the sacred
texts that have filled your mind with visions of a world that isn't
there. At the bottom of the web they are still waiting for a sign of
life from that poor doctor who has held her silly pose for hours,
much like Proust watching the specter of a rose fly straight out
of its bottle into heaven where it waits for a new forest to rise up
out of Siberia's great lakes.

For, Lo! She Is One Foot Too Short but She Gave Birth to All of Us

"It is the feminine heroic," Chloe whispers, soft as ash, her numbers all unharmonized. By now the birds have snatched their kisses from the Bolsheviks and grieving mothers surge into the foster homes to sow new lives with pandemonium.

But don't try skimming off the margins. While marathoners slow to watch the gondolas and tingle, your privacy disrobes. If it's a mystery that gets you feeling maidenform then we are here to wrinkle all your islands whether stern or richly sexed.

And, fluttering, they came like axioms or lilies with their petals torn, obscurely wandering through cities where mobs had trampled all of Chloe's grasslands in a rush to bulldoze mangy earthworks.

Negativity's deluxe nightmarishly pipetted. A mess of nips and tucks like Gaia bursting to give birth.

(Perhaps she was not tall enough.)

Groping Beyond the Landing Pad of Rote Multiplication

The old lady looked up and saw her classroom in a haze of loofah masochism. "Nibble nibble," said the shade of Ajax, grim and phallic, gagging shadows like a run-down tune, an edelweiss. Of course bullies stuck their tongues down through the great crevasse. They didn't know the tense or mood but Gaul was split into three parts. And then their little sisters spewed some nonsense they had clearly stolen from *The Wealth of Nations*. Summer students ate their lunch and left the stars to their stagnation. Spread upon a butcher's block, they could feel the acid rain eat through the window but they stopped their feeding long enough to hear the nurses croon lieder to the fatherland. Cells were multiplying. Soon they'd feel those tender spots of time float out of Egypt like Europa. Where the devil is the teacher when you need her? They are sensitive, these meadows. If you're quick, you'll catch a beetle, or a plastic bag and find that when you set them end to end they ring the earth a thousand times. Perhaps the plural. Portugal. Or an abalone abandoned to the quiet flux of sines and cosines as they open like the Red Sea. Balderdash. The dew point's edible and I'll be damned if even flies would make their nests amid this jargon. It's a brain, about to burst, monster trucks and endless ways to kill a blackbird

Stop, children, stop—Raphael has finished the maze!

Here's a Stone—How Will You Power It?

I think it must be obvious by now that no design could
account for all this darkness. When I say this I am speaking
to your phlegm, bones, bile, veins, and blood but not your face.
Those far-off, weeping Romans valued pain for its own sake.
They took great leaps (if sometimes backwards). "What's a body?"
they would ask the lonely Greekling as he stitched the sound of
his own name into an overcrowded sky (of course, we all know
it's not much beyond a source of metaphors but, then again, what
a relief to hear the old kook really *say* that). You can theorize
all you'd like but I won't let sluttish time dictate *my* private life.
This is *your* city. You can rent a plot to read your book and cry
about men who simply lie down quietly and die. Whether it's air
or fire you breathe, aim your questions beyond time and invoke
other writers only when they seem to swell the meadows, clad in
grasses, saying, "*This* is where *we* live, a place where, first, you see
its beauty, next, you see its speed and only then its alternations
and its interchanges." Do you really think the architects held out
their hands to petrify within the incense-smothered darkness,
driving laughter from their minds? *Domine,* I would not know.
It's just geometry, but when I say this I am speaking to your
armies and your ships, not to your cities. Here's a stone—how
will you power it?

How Mirthless the Panopticon without
Its Seven Wonders

Rain falls all lovey-dovey from a cloudless swab of sky and
sounds like heavy metal. There's little use in smiling
when Aegean blues refuse sublunary zen and drones are busy
hording our silver age's echoes.
Then, finally, it's naptime (speaking geologically).
    "I see you, dirty bird," the graying goddess lullabies.
Her hunger stuns the ghost of dialectic into spam (rhymes with
eternal life). We're sniffing out ambrosial anthems.
            Youth these days is so untimely, so we're stuck here
getting stoned on the panoply's encryption, still working on our
tans. The sunkissed hordes who murk the shadows know what it
means to hiss into a funk like Cleopatra.
Who will ask the perfect question?
                The Aegean, so aloof. Rachmaninoff's regret
all viscera & pockmarked. Stillness siphoned off the egrets.

How Not to Trust in Summer Rain

I held you to my heart.
      You were just so of the essence I could trace each
thrill of the sunset atomized, that is, the sun that never
happened.
The ropes we never tied vestigial as patterns yellowing upon
the walls.
      Your translucence is unnerving as the ocean smoothing
stones. A lifespan's slick isosceles displayed in heaps
  like bones. Behind the glass, decaying mammals scratch, sniff
and try to die, a small eternity fixed at the center of each
eye.
      And now the race is on with plants:
Pinching, pulling, burning, vicious.
Bodies sparked to life by a science so obscene the experts say
when someone's hurt they utter syllables that scrub the goodness
from all monotone.
      And so we scream.
Or maybe light a scented candle.

      That's right, my dove, distill a heart-shaped
foam quintessence. Nib yr. ur-lip squib n' chug.

How to Worship at the Throne of Abelard's Perversions

It's too late—your drunken tapestries will soon be
torn apart to line some nesting yuppie's cave. And the lilies
of Montmartre, too weak to say *adieu* to their master's vacant
stare will watch his happily-ever-afters grow right through the
atelier, now nothing but the whipping boys of torment, youth,
and hunger. We grab a fern and run. But the bourgeoisie's
outnumbered by the Matterhorn's reserve of firemen who fall in
place like drummer boys undressing for a vampire ball (electrodes
trailing from the bustles of their seamless marble gowns).
Tonight, mortality's assemblage will invite you to lie down and
play the timid guest to a Roquefort-bearing host.

        Contemplation cylinders revolve. Green spaces
encroach upon our half-hearted attempts to plug the fountain
with our fingers. The smell of *joie de vivre* brims from our
mushroom baskets. Speaking of the long-lost ancient forests,
we're tottering on stools carved out of solid Anglo-Saxon. But
some candle-licker cruel enough to break the spell has trimmed
our favorite vowels down to thuds. And if the sky erodes right
through? Then every missing crumb will echo the last gasp of
Nosferatu *en plein air* to extinguish Darwin's squalls.

        Silence! It's Charles Baudelaire, wrapping his cringing
mother in a ceremony scrawled upon some fallen virgin's tomb.
The modern era has begun!

        The little mishap slits her wrists and says the flowers
taste like meat.

        What a naughty pastime, love.
Now come and eat your stingy feasts!

I Was Just Killing Several Birds with My Impressionistic Prose

Some dull and plotted woodland action. It was, perhaps, just as we feared. Who would dare hazard the meaning of Lavinia in tears? Silence cruel as frozen water. Notebooks full of dust and sin. Remembering the dodo, we pause to let our thoughts inhabit other dioramas. You've told a monstrous lie and you'll soon learn how it feels to wrangle with your conscience trapped inside the tactile dome. That will be your last chagrin and now, to pluck a thorny question from this artless woman's chin. We have nothing to conceal. Suspicious packages arrive? Return to sender. Storm the exurbs. Let the lurid birds bedevil other archivists with their idiotic plans. I think her tears are real. Enough about the fauna. Watch the neighbors write their memoirs from atop the boundary stones. It's me but grey and faded and emerging from a poem. And, to think, that very morning, I was feeling so alive, watching the massive women toss their wickerware into the outer darkness, stony nipples sweeping straight across the tundra. Never mind. Put them away. Go play your small, dull, woodland dramas. I don't think her tears are real but I don't want to be the bitch to have roused you from your slumber. Ask the Kremlinologist if he thinks that high-pitched squeal is actually a sign of life. Flies titter round the studbook and the army takes all night to move a single, lousy stone. "Ah, lachrymose!" the expert sighs, watching the watchdog strain to brush some trees aside.

Ignore the Idiot Avenger's Sophomoric
Cries for Help

Ice doesn't lie. Well, no, it melts, and up spring automated sculptural tableaux studded with revolving doors and spiral stairs to calm our nerves with pointillistic dreamboat premises as we careen through effervescing seas of kelp. Either way, we should not speak but, rather, mouth newborn vowels like so much contraband barely waking from our naps. Eye-poppingly misrendered, the forlorn flower children trade monogrammed towels for rank tatami mats. Don't tell the metrosexuals there's nothing ergonomic about those flimsy screens. Infinity will cost you extra. But these morons have been *trained* to take you to the roof to see the dragonmaster. It's free so you pay nothing. When you look up you will see laws are labeled in linear B: *timeless themes.*
The professor turns his attention to dreams.

Imagining the Diacritics of the Next Great Death

The orphic owl's out of earshot and, in hindsight, we agree—that errant flikr was a feather, an eclipsed facsimile. The nimble art of deer-hoofed children fetchingly bedecked in purple trim, their pleasure zones igniting without anarchy. We are glum as islanders awash in beauty while sand creeps in like an overdose and deer eat from our hands. Coins and cups and cinderblocks accumulate upon our desks (they once belonged to pirates). So how can we resist this protoplasm fringed with saffron when the fetid facts caress our mercury through retrograde? Those awe-struck balls of flesh survived the saga, safe as shipwrecks, spreading good news to the ghosts. Uploaded in our consciousness, the afterimages compute the power of the pendant while a slow tornado sprawls its deadpan furthermost and emits one last hurrah. If these walls were more than grey they could explain it all, perhaps, while we stand on the burning deck hoping our sobs won't sink the ship.

In Memory of Those Who Died Before the Seas Could Part

You can go see them, their pink coffins nestled in the
flesh of magnolias waiting desperately to bloom while anger
in St. Petersburg eliminates the sun, our favorite star. They've
opened fire on the cold and unheard tongues of all the comfort
women flashing the signal to unlock the vaults of history.
What's left when every paradox fizzles out upon the luster
of a military swansong in the airport? Hours later they were
whispering denials that, at first, drew much applause from the
people walking by (agents of the borderland and allies of the
deer who grazed the clouds in hope of proving Virgil wrong.)
Their wings had caught on fire. The choreographers had learned,
whenever gunshots part the curtains people in the back row will
just synchronize their watches. Can't you feel them burn, caught
there behind the glass? Go on, recite hexameters about some
stranger drinking rivers from the mouths of exiled Kurds. In the
overcrowded prisons they're just waiting for the day to make
their great escape and plant new footprints on the moon. But the
deer who graze the sky look so darn golden and serene among
the flarf and doldrums. Cataleptic, well, perhaps, but, even dead,
the dictator was there to turn it into art: They dug his body up
and drove a stake straight through his heart.

Inside the Bleary Pyrotechnics of This Glass Menagerie

A beardless visage of eternity has oxidized our scheme of breaking through the firewall. And now the mizzen's taken wing on dirty pinions torqued to pulverize our ocean view. What's worse, tonight the fates fly down to snatch our maltepoo from beneath the dressing gown of sugary confection mother nature swathed her in. Despite the dimples, studies show you can't breed companionship into *el niño*. Boy, you snicker. But your sadness ricochets into the rock garden and triggers feelings of tranquility that coat the hemispheres like Snow White at room temperature. These days flatliners are slow to mist the grand rotunda with anything so sheer as "Once Upon a Summer Night in Prague."

Hydrangea, dear, don't spike the murky edges of the meltwater's meniscus. It will only leave you raw with googling, your freckles stitched into the fabric of a sky that shows no sign of blood. You'll type, "Do German Measles itch?" Do mute sensations hover like a jar of tsetse flies left out all night? The answer's no. And all the loving in the world won't make those tiny organs grow.

Too many questions left unanswered in the wake of Taffy's spin into the dark side (restless goblins sired by yappy synonyms). When will the villa misfits come to sanctify the bearded rose? Will the forget-me-not's mitosis traumatize the Shih Tzu? "Isn't she supposed to be bionic, funny mustaches aside?" spits the symbol-monger (now a real Victorian in her layers of dreamy lace shot through with cockamamie schemes). The little licker (Pekingese) ducks her face into the *crème brûlée* of the Atlantic and comes up seething jewels. So like a hyperactive saint you wouldn't take her for the foolish child of a dying Emperor's last indiscretion.

If a griffin is the only living thing you'll deign to mention you can take your pedigrees and crawl your way straight back to Malta where women speak in tongues of flame and children drown their polychromed tomorrows in the holy water.

Grinning soundlessly a lion streaks back through the abstract noun.

Instructions for Inhabiting a Miniature World

Somewhere in da Vinci's notebooks lies an earth that can't be flattened. When you find the fairy you must speak to him, in Latin. Demonstrate your expert knowledge of the forest and your urge to decorate his nook with odd-shaped, dimpled pearls plucked from the rings of widows. He will crinkle his small face. "But I am just a mannikin. I don't like playing games upon the bridge-too-far." Then you will disappear into the cool sfumato of his *vale* and things inside his leery gaze will twitch their iridescent horns. The inflection of his words will do a dance around the crude gleam of your evening English as it rusts in chunky piles. *Amo, amas, amat.* Flirtatiously, you'll try to utter sounds that will explode his world into abstractions. But all you have are nouns and birds torn from the sky by winds so strong they turn the recto into verso: a rabbit's foot, a lake of blood, a root system that dives below the underbrush to penetrate the forest floor bidding us to join the revels in extended metaphors.

Jeremiah Says She Doesn't Like Androgyny

There's no need to rust up that old SUV with a trip
to the dark side. The whole partybarn's in a dither, revved up
by the shape of your dress. Kitty-wampus, my love, you are so
Rorschachesque. I can feel you aligning the magnetic fields with
your scrollwork, as astral as unquarantined. But edelweiss blooms
right here on the ground. And this Byzantine lurch is too lonely.
Come down and we'll skid on the inchoate gap that's eroding our
missa solemnis, our fingers and toes so small you can't count them
as ornament—yet they're completely organic. How pale we will
be as longitudes stretch and strum efflorescing the limberlost's
curls and the rose windows burst with indolence, sad as a *fait
accompli.* Stop looking away—you're not even crying. And I've
learned by heart every inch of new growth, carving stone into
flame like a nun without hope of ever unbinding asymmetry's
marvels. And there you will be, still ghosting my novel, a small
purple patch the heroine dreads to ever encounter in mixed
company.

Laughing Our Way Out of the Structure of the Joke

Freud belongs, but in the footnotes. In the meantime, face your fears. I've been google stalking you for 16,000 years without quite knowing what I'd do if your silent face should swim up from the middle distance. But I've only found vague traces of your twin (a mathematician who reserves her brightest smiles for the blondes down at the tiki bar. She has been sharing files with the forest people. All 5,000 of them fit quite comfortably inside her hard drive. Scrolling down through the expanding alphabet I come upon a petty chief who swears his coat of arms is not a monster but a beast whose single golden horn traced a path across the Alps long before the word "sublime" ever unbarred a pilgrim's mouth). She said, let there be light. I think if all of us survive we should forget the laboratory, put the wagon in reverse and make for the Sierras like the Swedes who thought they'd find gold nuggets in the mountains and then did. They bought the house next door to my apartment. They believed in something. Fine. But we're here sifting through the only archive we can find, pressing delete when we get angry at people or rain spreading like melancholy handshakes. Missing pages of Montaigne lie scattered on your desk in a vague pattern that reveals how the rotation of your mind has shaped the earth's magnetic field. But, in the end, we're not clairvoyant. And we can only poke so many holes into ether without laughing.

Lecture on Organic Form

What's left of a glass body when the glass is swallowed whole for its abstract, fragile beauty? Pouring water into forms that leave no fear behind them, only freedom not to blast artifacts from their museums. The curator had shaped them softly with her science but their symmetries were gone before they'd hardened into wisdom. And the lecturer just droned about the scars that marred their beauty. The pages seemed to quake with fear or was it recognition? He drained a vase and asked if anyone had any questions. A small tree seemed to show some interest in the fearsome metaphors he'd used to illustrate their power. A massive cat had draped its prey across the branches. A wan girl in the back row gave a quiet little shiver as the water spread its wake across the vastness of the topic. That smell would linger long after the metaphors lost track of the traumas they'd endured inside their gruesomely masked bodies. Perhaps it's better not to know if sounds have moral feeling. Ahem. Off-topic. So the speaker dug into the dirt, extracting liquid snow.

Lie Quiet, Divus. . . .

Visiting Kyoto's temples, Malatesta's junk shop, parts pulled from an archetypal sentence. Well-known scholars have remarked that modern heroism is a riddle but the gods are bored of living thus. Really, you should learn the art of catching dreams more slowly. Leave monuments to seep in azure, oedipal. Solipsistic winters' nights of breathing human subjects into statues are no more. And scholars just remind you of your mother heaping stones into a sinking ship, unconscious of her crimes.

Old Verona's full of spirits (how Catullus would have roared with laughter from the cockpit as your molten English slid across the margins of his ugly adolescence). But the tug of only speaking when you're spoken to is just too strong. And though you've never tasted blood, I do believe you may have seen it rising in the eyes of other diplomats. A centaur's single leg hangs like an unsolved crime and life goes on, the days outstretched upon their weary scaffolding. If muscles train the mind then we must climb. Lord Elgin, please, we've had enough of your advice. Well then, back to the ship! You'll have to sweep the middle distance for some other Artemis and send the wax casts back to China with Lolita. Never mind. I no longer have someone to love and hate at the same time so save your drama for the footnotes and just let me weep a bit. Those may be tears but this is glass shed with exquisite craftsmanship.

Life-Lessons Gleaned from a Grammar
of Attic Inscriptions

Ampersands entwined the alpha waves like revelations.
She was turning ten years old and so she practiced levitation in the hope
that soon the cosmic egg would crack, the rusty air unleash its dragon
robes and a glossary of wonders written when the ancient world was
still miraculous would fold eternities of breathing into a lifework lush
enough to coax a human face out of the velvet tiger's jaws.

Just then, a bluebird

(happiness) fanned the fires of dawn in search of surfaces to
saturate with molten colors. We filled our perfume bottles with the
sound of creamy letters dripping, marbleized, into a blackened pool of
contradiction. Ceremonial as swords, her guest-friends made a fiction
out of every object. Bored, the farmers shook their heads. "We're gonna
have some weather," they muttered as the cracked earth rived their
Camelot. Their wives, like pitchforks, muttered back.

And the bluebird

(happiness) tried to swerve inland and cheat them of their rage
(automatons! with real bugs in their beaks!) while their husbands raked
the earth for azurite turning their backs on their beloveds tearing pages
from flaming almanacs.

Time for the tiramisu!—then true happiness will scroll our local
mini-Mozarts through its limpid diastole. The bluebird clatters through
a mazy corridor and, blitz!: We're entering the private chambers of a
well-known humanist. But the windows are so dirty and the ceiling is so
low it has snuffed our only candle. He tries to genuflect.

I suppose you girls grow tired swimming in that inland ocean.
And the eyelids of your clones are not yet strong enough to open.

And the bluebird

(happiness) is so oblivious.

His feathers flare like dragons turned away toward an eternity
together.

Long Live the Little Lady's Need to Construct Her House of Glass under the Sign of Debussy

This blanched meridian is just a temporary structure
the builders left to rust at the edges of the Alps. So now, it's
wilderness or bust your budding revolution on a grim minority
of little princesses (children of botany whose tender spirit worlds
will bring the clock towers of industry's confusion crashing
down. They thrush in loutishness always peering toward the
center where faded colors run. They smelt their anger into crowns
of limp grandiflora then run back to the beach, a herd of would-
be ballerinas, overglutted by the chic of moonlight massacres.
They shun the very scent of love. You'd think the *nachtmusik* had
never bathed the barricades in blood).

But, of course, you all know better. For you have read
the book and chronicled the archway's opalescent blight, from
thwarted Visigoths to the walls of Père Lachaise. Can't you see
it's spritzing in the garden of the blessed?

Ten more years of heavy labor and a gastronomic sludge
will surge up from the crypts to engulf our fear-stained cowls.
Then we will haunt the Hall of Mirrors hearing nothing but
the king's lush, whimsical amalgam echoing off velvet walls
in the kingdom's inner sanctum, baffling the engineers: it's a
computerized fountain shedding real live human tears.

Misty-Eyed Manhattan Contemplates
the Golden Age

Nature tells us she abhors free gifts. Hard to believe? That slut still haunts the waterways of Gotham masked in shades of sky blue nubuck. Haunts the frozen waterways. Hard to believe? The city shares her silence with the rainmakers. My friend, I'll comb your hair until streets unbind the sleepers and iron gates slam shut trapping our hieroglyphs like pinions. Touch the touchpad. Pins drop. Up above, the sky, caressed by islanders, unlocks collective stares. Afraid of airborn viruses, the child prodigy prepares a shield of petrochemicals he'll use to seal his room off from the street noise. Have you heard? These streets are melting but the moon's refused to leave her winter garden. Can we help it if we miss the sound of other animals? Their greedy hands and feet have turned our virgin forests into arbors. If his room becomes too small, the child shivers. We've all been taught this gloom is just the rasp of charlatans writing prescriptions while snow falls lightly over Brooklyn in remembrance. But who knows, the streets might not, in fact, be golden and your hair might have escaped its knots to become tangled in the jealous hands of Fate, a woman who cannot be silence even when the child burns his books crying that life has ruined everything he's learned.

Mundane Cloudscapes Threaten
the Organic Metaphor .

Djin monkeys lolling in the aftermath of a parade,
grandeur and decline just empty shapes the mouthparts made as
many-sided messages of gladness pierced them through. Emote
like manga, bleeding nectar. Well, in hindsight, we all knew the
fourteenth-thousandth generation would still hunger and still
thirst. It's just that, now, the water's wetter. Total darkness never
hurt as much as this agog enlightenment. Refresh. Renew. The
other puzzlemakers try to nestle in the folds of cosmic brouhaha.
But, floor-to-ceiling, stacked debris. Emanating from an apple,
hair-thin lines run through the third eye, skyward. In the air, a
divine gas, the curse of history uploaded in a podcast while cells
divide inside our hearts alert, alive, and glistening. So there's
nothing more to fear, right, Doc?
　　　The doctor wasn't listening. He was counting alpha waves
as they gauged his private beach, cursing softly as vague fish
plucked at the surface of the deep.

New Worlds Are Just Around the Bend
My Neoplatonists

You'll see the icons, lacerated into plausibility, escaping from their niches, running wild through a scene collaged from soft Italian suede, awash in Botticelli Green. You'll see satyrs dancing barefoot and mathematicians blinded by your wild daisy skirts stretching points into straight lines with such grim mindfulness their beards begin to fall like snow, like frozen breath, like some archangel. And only then will the sun set upon the ledges to dangle from trees its leaky wetware vulcanized. The lurid sums and colors lure boys to the bordello where women slake their thirst with crude meanders. A reminder: The inventor of this curse knew nothing about magic so bring on the next disaster. "But look, my wounds have healed." My god, foreverafter's just a nocturne played at noon, a Dutchman telescoping time into a single Roman candle! The tyranny of rhyme slinks in like some Medusa nearly hypnotized with laughter. There are distances that no good Platonist should try to master.

No One Hears You Laughing at Yourself Inside That Marble Cube

The sky is a featureless white and the children can't
be bothered to grow older. They are wiser than they look. They
picked the locks of this forbidden city years ago and now they
are just lost trash burning, earning points by barely being here
legislating the decay, outlawing evening walks among the endless
miracles and facts that hold up half the sky while lightning
streaks across the streets into the end-zones. Why should we
be severed from the science of a system that has laced even the
giant forests into its mechanics? Where the roots gape open our
inventions will illuminate the halls and we will find new crevices
to fill with choruses and we will call our new lives by new names
the names of mountains that have grown too high to house
a spirit who might hear us. That great wall is there to shield
you from the animals who fled the scene and lost themselves
(unschooled in Mandarin, they thought the brand-new city
blocks were featureless and white, great hunks of marble lucidly
absorbing all the tremors that the earth made as vans and people
moved upon it. In the meantime, we must walk without touching
anything through these new cities, for our skin would stain the
beauty of the stone). The athletes, barely stripped of all emotion,
pour themselves straight through the living rock. Not even a
small splash. And never the warm tears they want to shed—their
bodies are still changing shape. Their breath is just a path for
sediment and shadow to escape through while sirens probe the
night's immortal diamonds looking for immortal diamonds.

Now Hush—You're Not Melting, You're Caught in the Glow of His Majesty Resting in Child's Pose

I remember the face of each low-riding thug fighting down disbelief in the morning doves, skirting their orbiting rims, eliciting cries. Lead dapples their beaks. The messenger tries to announce that the air is too thin. "Getting thinner is like getting high!" snores the pink-bellied swimmer whose scatterbrain murks that wintry isle (Mute lessons in mother-of-pearl). All the while we sit in the shade of his fossilized throne shouting, "Long live the king!" (Though we know he is stone deaf, dumb, bad in bed, and dwarfed by the blur of our scallywag mouths). So much left unread as the smooth backing peels from the hedges and sticks like a murderous grub to the exit signs. All the blood's rushed to our heads, we can feel the ground cracking. Our vacuum-packed cushions sink straight through the earth. We've shrink-wrapped our last bit of chintz and rested like shrubs in the backwash of warm violins. But, alas, no rebirth. And our heart-rates have slowed to an ambient shrug. But that's how it hurts when the keyboards dissolve and glass-blowers blow whole fountains of ash through your kingdom of snow.

Now to Release the Birds of Prey to Haunt Some Other Inland Sea

      Our Scout inspects the false interior. He checks the shag for hairs and puts the soundtrack on repeat. The Maltese falcon wouldn't dare reveal its horde of secrets to such a taskmaster. He knows that, if the slipknot loosens, he'll find comfort in the chill of communism's empty halls. The slipknot loosens—fetish, famine, foe, realpolitik. These walls will only crush his mind beneath a force, like gravity, that is both slow and everywhere. Soldiers drift in like dead leaves still clinging to the stem of their enveloped firmaments. Was it so wrong to reach our hands through the interstices? There are no victims left. These rooms are emptier than graves and cold as synthesizers. Put your contact mic away. We've blazed our trails. We've built our fires. If the center doesn't hold we'll simply have to close the blinds and let the objects decompose.

Our Day Spent Overturning Urns Inside the Columbarium

Adrift on seafoam-colored bathmats woven from recycled rope. Many perish. The survivors scan the fallacies of hope their dramas junglelike until a jingle slowly plumes from an adjoining island. Turning, awestruck, from this new catastrophe, we drag our shattered bodies toward the beach, trailing wire, silk, and shocks. Embalmed in snowflake-patterned fleece, the elders ban all further mention of missing engineers. Warmth without wetness? Tell the fashionistas we are not prepared to lose our lives so quickly. We confess, we told our brood of look-alikes their hunger wasn't sexy. Baby, who remembers back that far? The sea malingers. We are ringed with fire—fifteen minute flunkies of the monkey king. We rush the waves, alive, if hobbled slightly by our skinny jeans. Beauty by mail. It's free. Surrender. Feel it tingle up your seams. Yes, we are lost, but like a wingéd boy, in search of endless summers, our blind eyes shed blue tears to shock Van Eyke out of his slumber.

Phantom Etymologies of the Ides of March

Caesar could take his little finger, lift it deftly to his head and
bring a room of soldiers to their knees.
Effeminacy's dead. ·
Why was it wonderful? The Whistler gals are lovely pale but, like
your mom, they are too gloomy.
Four p.m.. It's time to share your thoughts with all your friends,
who's first? Oh me! me! me! I'm sick of all the pagans and their
polyamory. Well I say no! no! no! to insects singing without
words. Frankly, the trees (our ur-umbrellas) are too flimsy.

Oddment, funk, spud awkward as our hero tries to poke
fun at the shapelyness of movement. He clasps his gyroscope
and bores a gimlet hole into the zeitgeist that will seep like an
old lizard through the cockney—*eins, zwei, drei!*—the corkscrew
brandished like a candlestick its blue flame almost lovingly intent
upon the patch of grass beneath the sundial.
The cement has settled. And, Augustus, you are with us
but these shabby pigs disturb the *pax*. They say your uncle
was unnerved by such grammatical disjunctions. He liked his
proper nouns to sit politely in the senate house. (Their murder
instruments were rustling in the silence, something lost and far
from home).
The *imperator* was distracted by a lizard and he raised his finger
to the lithe and slimy patch of cells that fringed his head: *Et
tu Brute?* Radiating Hollywood. Of course, he said it best in
Shakespeare, where his mimsy was a sherd of trilobite, his om
the saddest music in the world. But, was it really wonderful, the
vortex wondered, dead! dead!! dead!!!?

Ideas bleed green and ever rustling murder, edible.

Rimming the Pacific

I suppose I could have jumped. Instead, I flirted with
an inkling, mumbling angelically, "The kitten only has one eye."
Flubbed ordinary tasks (our kvetching bloomed straight on the
kisser.) Rooms the size of children's teeth evacuating monks.
To journey, emberlike, across a hairless nipple tipped with life as
varicose as dreamwork's Ptolemaic fracture. It's like sure, *vavoom,*
you know. Does staring make us sinners? Despite its lack of rigor,
the moonlight gave us lumps. Just stop and think, my pretty, that
exile-owned hooray where they teach you about gender, then
stuff you full of sex is just a coy echolocation, a splurge against
the goons who widen children's eyes with sheets of candy shaped
like oil.

We converted harum-scarum fractal duty, timely slaughter,
and then wrapped it up in sheer and clung—*as if* (for, suddenly,
the air, all jelly, felt too tender to hedge an arctic purge, so we
touched without our mittens).

Thank god the kid had wings and the air was fairly
roomy. Our pleasures hung like gardens crystallized among the
heathens. Another runic beard burst loudly through the crypt.
But the horse's heads were doomed to years of fuzzy thinking.

She Fluttered Through the Room Where I Was
Talking with Frau K

I have named the sparrow Dora. I am keeping her alive.
She's stubborn and indifferent but I'm patient and I've tried to
thread her like a fire beneath hidden doors saying, "Enter at
your own risk to watch axioms engorge our wisdom like a winter
without love while, underground, fossils make dark quips and
crack as little Dora frowns her way straight into limbo rudely
licking up the yolk." What is your favorite species? In the dead of
night you speak as though this great experiment were neither sad
nor strange. Your overactive superego's interfering with our fame.
Its shadow hulks across this page. Its sadness slaps us like a lie
told to avoid a mother's fury. Wherever did she find the courage
to unravel those unseemly archetypes beneath the shadow of a
kirk? Creep creep. The insects pry their way into our story with
a battery of calls: *Ennui, ennui.* Don't listen! Blast those critters
from the walls and let brave Dora lick her lips. The doctors hang
their heads in shame watching each bird evolve into an echo of
her name.

60 Degrees Outside but It's Still Snowing
at J.Crew

Would you like to fuck the cashmere, I can go start you
a room. "No thanks, just looking," upchucks the *nom de plume*
all pink beneath her camisole and bright-eyed as the breeze.
Just warm breath on a window pane. You call that company?
Well, at least *I* have a noisemaker and *I* know what to do
when those steamy druids get all atmospheric. Crush them by
reverse osmosis! Bus in geophysics geeks to wax poetic about
Stonehenge! If the ghostwriters repeat themselves *ad infinitum*
just relax, enjoy the show. Stars link us directly to the ancient
past. What's so inviting about data when you can't even compute
the circumference of this shibboleth? God help me, I will shoot
the next person who tries to sell me on a shade of green I can't
even pronounce. Hyperbarbaric, baby. Please, don't liquify
the salesgirl. It's not her fault that love has no hypotenuse.
Sometimes they call it seaside chic but I prefer to search the atlas
for more subtle clues, not signs of the apocalypse. No worries.
Cowboy jeans may be the newest kind of sexy but they don't
quite fit. You know, the lights we see today may well have burned
up years ago.

Soon We Will Sing in the Voices of Angels but Don't Hold Your Breath

An eagle slithers off its coin into the waiting hand of
God. We spoon, magnetically, and freeze there, stunned by the
applause. And soon a chilly nimbus glyphs congealing lushness
with a burst of newborn computations. A stutterer's c-c-c-
curse resounds through the bright night to seep like damp into
the bones of waiting refugees. Deep inside the astrodome our
hazy flight toward new desires flares up with a sudden whisper
or a faint, metallic glint to mutter, "If you love her, kiss her."
Sentiment to flood the sperm bank with remembrance of beds
unmade by mother love. Sure enough, the bald spot spreads
straight through the seraphim where molten clouds get tangled
up in Shanya's parachute. She hits the ground in Arkansas, her
failures scaring the bejesus out of the theatre crowd who take her
for a readymade. She's only lost six teeth and smiles.

In the mountains of Kashmir a missing body's been
recovered. Dead white beneath its burqa, the pink canary
shudders.

Suggestions for Transporting Glass-Paned Polyhedrons

A flock of beveled birds invades the learning lounge. Go, Elijah, shake your fist. We're seeking higher ground. The cheetah spots us climbing piles of sand, our footprints shaped like dust. His claws retract. We hesitate, afraid our movements won't be natural enough to break the spell. On cue we laugh out loud. Take the moment by the cuff! Rip out the centerfold! But who has time to read for pleasure in the midst of all this fauna? My dear, I stand corrected, this evening's docudrama must unfold without beasts, they've gone extinct and I have spent the best years of my life trying to tame them. In the end we'll all just melt away inside these chambers bleeding rust upon a frozen, lifeless world. But if you tough it out for one more half-life you can watch your real emotions scrawled with glitter pens across the strand. Our inner goddess paws the earth, she'd like to spend another evening with the Shah (he is now warm and optimistic in his huge, synthetic parka shooting emails to the world below, each nanosecond split into a thousand vaulted ceilings. Illusions that will break through even shafts of sun, bright as a fountain made of Farsi, translucent as a boy who demons teach to dip his pen into the darkness, flex his muscles, and ignite the highways with his filthy debt to the Valley of Light).

Sunken and Odorless as Sappho's Garlands Seeped in Argon

"Wraith and rapture!" said the master in high German as he tied eternal sentences, now rendered cryptic by the flies that gather in such weather, into a maudlin "Oh" with a chilled and useless flourish. Please don't leave us here alone. Inside the fledgling opus, Don Pedro plucks a plum from the dark side of the meadow. Its materials dissolve impeccably and other objects are revitalized by this new show of strength. We wipe our bleary souls—on what? Books left unread? Each quiet page will turn translucent and the author's hand, now visible, will burn its lingering aspersions into the lapsing—snuff those dreary wastes, your spirit world, drowned girl, is not enough! Lie still, my fair-cheeked faun and listen closely: your despair is but a soft, iambic beat shedding treasures through the air's forgetful, long goodbyes—its tragedy struck dumb as flowers forced to bow their heads and kiss the hand that plucked them.

The Blind Leading the Blind Inside a Crystal Cave

Once you start looking at spiders there's no turning back. The years web into one another and it's hard to really know whether lightning falls in waves or particles. Clutching their medals to their chests marathoners shave another hour off the mile. But the rest of us are slow to recognize their triumph, dragged around the world with twenty hours to go before a massive fireball descends to sway the laws of gravity. The boys have built a maze to mitigate our boredom as we sit here growing old, too tired to prowl the open market for that heart of gold the radio had promised. But the calculus displaced our fears of finitude and let us glide off into space bearing the names of all rich men and their mothers and their wives and their sullen teenage children while a hand invisibly unthreaded Christmas lights and all the honeybees dropped dead, their burdens dusting the exhumed acanthus leaves with something close to pleasure (though it wasn't quite polite of the officials to decapitate their king). So many lights. Which one will burn out first? I guess I should have known my life would end this way but we arachnophobes are only vague and sentimental—oh the things we might have said if there were world enough and time. Sunlight vanishes and the tree-sitters wave banners, shedding clothing through the dark. I don't know about those canopies, but I do know this park is dangerous past dusk. Some day the trees will grow so tall that nothing new will grow beneath them.

The Dance That Held Our City Captive is Now Nursing Thunderbolts

Petrushka's other lover, afraid of death by water, has fled into a cityscape believing that his fortune is interred in the foundation of a house that seems to drift, each night, a little closer toward the Island of the Blessed. There are as many doors as prizes and he knows that every time he turns a corner, he can open one and witness the revenge of would-be soldiers who are stuck at home without their guns. But he'll never once change color, even as he grows quite bored of the mesmerists whose jokes reverberate straight through the crowd gathered at the door hoping one day to catch sight of the beloved as he tests his brand new pair of wings. We shall leave him orbiting the Emerald Necklace and imagining a future in which time no longer envies youth. We are sure the parting ship will leave a trail of stories circulating in its wake. History is in the making while they fleck bits of paint off the foundation and look up at stars that never once change color. "Twinkle, twinkle, little bat" a befuddled Sergei mutters as he thinks about those little ladies with their swimming eyes and thick, adoring laughter. The beloved is now basking in the glory of his strength. Yes, he is worshipping the sun, arched into a perfect cobra and letting his forked tongue slither beyond the snip of fate. Let us watch his hair cascading through the cosmos for a moment and then leave his love to wade back through the arctic lake where our hero spent his youth admiring his mother. If those waves could only reach the beach to curse the countess just imagine what they'd say (She played the fiddle while Rome burned and then she simply walked away).

The Day Your Tattooed Ship Capsized Inside My Tattooed Tear

As a fan of Wonderbras and as an Anglophone, I'm smitten by your obelisk, my dear. But when a stone butch speaks, you listen, saving your shadowboxing for another day. Her tears were cold and thick as milk. Her eyes were glistening with strangled legends of the old days when filched petunias nestled in their scabbards, grim and phallic. Can't you smell them? Baby, listen, I was saying something thick and deep and delicate as glass blown for a chapel window. I was torn between incalculable sadness and a mundane lump of snowy fear. One day, we'll liquify Las Vegas. For now, I'll whisper in your ear a tale of seedy calques and fleeting pulchritudes. Now that I've cashed my mother's check, I'll drop out of the school that taught me better than to idolize so utterly. Go ahead then, cowgirl, plunder. Rip the pages from our book and plunge your greedy hands into another tragic scene. The Renaissance is waiting. Distant waterfalls will carry our emotion straight across that ragged border. We'll confront our *faux amies,* enchant the dyke march with our orderly accounts of life and death (true tales from underneath the knife). Osiris, Isis, resurrection . . . Mademoiselle, tonight let's throw perversion to the stars and preach unto the choir. Love is hanging in the balance. But the English never tire of politely knocking: *Please sir. Could you? Oh my word. Too kind.* Go on, love, eat your princess cake. A girl cannot subsist on rhyme.

Empty Space Is Vast Inside the Cells of Human Wit

Did you hear the flames fall silent, intercepted like a blurb returning from a country not quite ready for new words? The experts say good riddance. Let them eat their cake and split their atoms. Tenderfoot and her poetic waxing kit just didn't have the glow-how. Empty things are vast and slow inside this trumped-up cloud's erasure. As an expert I should know how not to read your silences but then you smile and I trip over a pile of descendents. They gasp and I can guess, in that grey moment, that the tremors I had felt were not your hands reaching out in bare survival but your heartbeat. Here we stand casting our shame into the fog and shouting straight out of the blue, "I am a son of joy! I do, I do, I do!" Do what? Declare the sky off limits and the ships an emanation of the mind. Don't try to keep that riddle secret.

The Graphics Smear and Raw Transcendence Spreads Its Ugly Jaws

Miracles do happen but don't hold your breath. What are we supposed to do, japanimate ourselves to death while doe-eyed misfits hop their Jettas ripped and ready for the slaughter? The Terminator takes the reins, whipping the ocean's daughters into a frothy mess and, lo!, blind fish float up dead and tired of brimming toxic thoughts. All right then, let's compute how many macromolecules it takes to stud a gargoyle's chest with infomercials. Nada. Pure enigmas split the roof in cosmic sympathy with every eyelash that blinks by. The sands of time are seeping through the windows and our lives become just that much smaller. Things we might have said if we had rimmed the earth's circumference are just passing fads. The dead can crawl out of their graves for all I care. There are no laws that say our technicolored dreams can't fade. The lion lets his paw drag back behind him in the dust, searching for reasons to abhor the vacuum. He refuses to let its watchmen roar "Go Bears!" wearing the vestiges of planets on their heads. The graphics smear—my god, it's true, we're not in Kansas anymore.

The Insomniac's Hollywood Mineralized

On *les grands boulevards* the true theatre is grieving: The
Venus de Milo's internal bleeding has soaked through her sheets
and stained the whole bed with *crème de cassis*. It leaves a big "If"
embalmed in deep space where private eyes wager on who will
come clean up the mess. Out in nature the patient exhales and
the tree of life strips the last of its leaves just in time for the flight
of a tin hummingbird—the first of the season! A sign sent by
Ovid to air out this prison and gather the steam of our lover's last
breath. Just look at the Sphinx in her thoughtlessness. So, gentle
reader, we write as aerosol spray disinfects a new dawn with its
faint *tra-la-la*. Now the wan alphabet of the dung beetle draws
us through Isthmian flights. Greta Garbo was wrong. Love, the
screens aren't so big. Myth-makers have trapped us in memories
of days when our faces weren't smashed into diamonds of light
and when hermes lined the paths now clotted with stars with
their lewd namelessness.

The Orchidologist Draws Yet Another Dirty Look from the Hermaphrodite Whose Petals Fringe This Curious Old Book

Another hothouse suicide. The old taxonomies have strained beyond the nocturne's wherewithal. Polypeptide chains delight in meditative music. "How quixotic," says the drudge, running his great divining rod 'round a quintessence. Tides of sludge and we have hooked a dreamless creature, its sterile blinks bejeweled until the third eye opens, a new dimension blooming through the great crepuscular that wreathes our empty shore, its fringed labella valedictions through the hypertext. Once more we're plucking the wings off angels. Their empty mouthparts throng to gather last remains into their folds. But a sarong's geometry is nothing sacred. Suicidal, yes, and doomed to sipping nectar. Yet it might exceed our ciphers. Then the moon can wax and wane and wax again for all we care. Scatter dust while we descend into a cavern where they cannot bury us.

The Painted Tiger Tiger Hates His Symmetry and Fights His Way out of the Frame to His Creator's Great Delight

There goes the nameless wonder shopping naked for new pets. It's enough to freeze the nipples off a marble statuette. Chip the teeth out of her mouth, paint her with gaudy reds and blues, look down at her in pity and she'll just stare back as though the revolution never happened. Never mind. We're in the path of the tornado but our little dog's so happy scampering through Kansas City in full color watching buildings rise and fall. Trapped inside his plastic sphere, my hamster's too enthralled by hints of chamber music to rise up toward the light emanating from the mask of the marquis. Take back the night you random fountain jets and wan reflecting pools. Pop some melatonin, turn back time, go back to school or face the future like a grace note while the good witch, all in white, flies off to dig new species from the forests of the night.

The Polymath's Achtung

Your riveting stigmata won't suspend our wanderlust. A neon sign deep in the desert says, "Your time is important to us," and we believe this *schadenfreude* to the point of self-hypnosis, spinning each imperfect night into an infinitesimal calculus of Saturns, Neons, Camrys, Jettas, Voyagers and *bling!* That's right Bob, no more microsleeps. Just gasoline psychosis and Bella Dancerella mastering her former lives into a moonshaped space or lune. There, there, my anomie, I know it's hard to keep your shirt tucked neatly in with all these zounds hammering their dulcimers and infernal draperies hanging limp as bad Claymation in the histrionic sun. Does that explain why South Koreans are trimming their tongues?

(She lit a cigarette trilingually and tried for once to just enjoy herself. "Barely barely velveteen" she said to coax her inner orphan from beneath the alpine sprawl. We cheered the impossible triumph of it all.)

It was a clammy arboretum warm with tiki prints warping the laws of nature into something more deranged than what aging physicists mumble from their podiums: *Feathers, giggles, nymphs, nymphs, nymphs!* (They are writhing from their frames!)

"Wait just a bloody minute," the bathing beauties cried, "these nightwatchmen are synched up to the rhythm of the tides and our most abnormal cravings are nothing but a hiss of nonsense syllables unbound and glad to be alive exploring Copenhagen's indigent blues. Such a long journey to end up in this empty petting zoo with Morpheus' dry lips euthanizing our elation. How would you like to have that happen on *your* mystery vacation?"

You could have snapped the silence. No cathecting. We were stumped. But the image was delicious, so boneless and dry: a shard of the vast ice our children would cross in search of better light to read their cataclysms by.

The Road of Excess Leads to the Palace
of Wisdom

My favorite kinds of calculation are symmetrical. They fit (if darkly) in the hollow of all multiples of six. I find such combinations beautiful. I love to see them etched in giant circles, seeking fire. When I think about these numbers I see Icelandic gardens where memories of youth lie raw and pebble-like upon a nest of smoother shapes. Such soft, white words surround us. When one begins with T it's often orange like a tulip. I close my eyes and sip a frozen river as it cracks into seas of textured colors. Into flocks of geese. Into sounds of pain. Neurologists might like the birds but I like five (a clap of thunder) also Wednesday (a blue word but a very pointy number).

The Sheik of Araby's Mechanical Burlesque

"Sabine's a diplomatic nightmare in crescendo today," sighs the Master of Puppets. Ah, *cirque du soleil!* Let me listen to your golden voice or be a new-sewn swan adrift upon the gelid perfection of a professional ice pond. Unfurl the technicolor dreamcoats! Roll out the iron lung! Threadbare illusions streak the night in spider web appliqué. In the back row ill-bred children hawk lugies in the hush of bristling prosthetics. *Voilà,* the Griffin Twins have just arrived to atomize your feathery cocoon with pornographic laughter. That niacin flush will not save you from monotony's undulant regression, never mind the fond hereafter: *Au clair de la lune* the iceberg shrinks back from its shadow. As blue light turns to red new friends cross-pollinate and shrouded ladies fill the tunnel with the sound of *Stille Nacht.* They touch stars with their bare hands.

"Come over here!" they cry. Joy echoes through no-man's land.

The Shiftless Art of Watching Dead Things Rising at the Louvre

The Birds of Paradise have grown beyond the reach of man, emitting chartreuse cries along the esplanade. The sands of time have worn so thin, landlocked oarsmen cannot see them shift to fill our gowns with evening aetiologies.

Slipped beyond this breach of science, a hermaphrodite, perplexed by moonlight monoliths, distilling absent-mindedness like some anonymous Diana sipping chardonnay, removes her pallium. Mid-April's unimpressionistic moods pattern the gallery with thought-experiments whose frames defy the ancient law that keeps the painted clouds from raining.

"Shove it down your fluted throats." How cruel and ladylike they ram beyond the reach of reason. In a perfect world the flaming of their surfaces would soothe the Satyr's beveled tongue. You wouldn't need to hold my hand. But, look, more visitors have come to touch the face preserved in wax. And tomorrow they will sigh, "Cede to the pleasure of your spectators!"

The dying slave revives long enough to wring his hands. The gallery is smothered in a fog of instant ash. Slit through the marble, verdant plumes. Then, numbingly, sensation!
A memory clings like an epithet's embrace to sink right back into stone.

The slave imagines himself mastered by the angel-maker, bruised then rising like a blasted tree or ebbed, unbuttressed, from the blue.

The Sour Easter Feast of Madame Butterfly

Behind curtains fluttered rumors of another golden
child. The concertmeister's faintly crass, metallic smile unnerved
the heaving body as they drew it toward the blade, its shouts
still trapped inside. Would the chrystanthemums obey the
voice that told them not to leak their secrets? No—her death
was mostly quiet and its melody deferred to the last breath as
it withdrew into a private room backstage. Just then, two white
kimonos glided up onto the ship that would, with any luck, be
sailing toward the sun now rising modestly upon their ritual.
But it had come to seem ridiculous, outdated, like a name kept
long after you've grown into a dark-eyed child who frowns each
time her captain even mentions butterflies. Its wings were wildly
unrhythmic. The prong stuck down her throat and swayed there
as servants took obligatory bows. Untie the blindfold, darling.
Withdraw into the hum of apathetic swords and catastrophic
flares. Untie the blindfold and the sun will still be sitting there
right where you left it as the canopy of screams rolls on and on
warmed by the florid breathing of the fading eidolon.

The World's Imagined Corners Curl in Answer to Our Prayers

From across the great divide an ancient miscellany stirs. Its gloomy poker face heaves in an effort to be heard above the trumpet-blasts. A dust has settled on the sun. Desolate, if wide awake, Saskatchewan's chilled sarcophagus rears round the swollen edges of a newborn continent traumatized by thunder. Those stormy malcontents plumbing the fossil record for a peccadillo. Who can blame them when the air's so silent and longitude runs slipshod through an undiscovered forest full of words so unpronounceable the newborns laugh amid their furs and hug the Ivory Coast. The rumor spreads: a golden child. Islands dripping vital fluids. Now that francophiles have settled down to sleeping with the philosophs we'll tune our pitchforks to the spheres and ask the natives to seduce the night with glottal stops. They think our dances slovenly. But they'll still join us (we're all stuck here, underneath the same big moon). This mound-building's contagious and the mountain-passes speak of further labor in the hinterlands. Alarmingly, we've reached the limits of remembrance emulsified as facts stitched in cuneiform and flowing from an hourglass. "Come, taste these algorithms." The system-builders bleach the bones out of our bodies as we stretch upon the strand waiting for miracles to surge up from the sea, desperate to hack our way out of deep play's cacophony.

Time to Ozonate the Plants and Make Them Come Alive

Don't worry, doctor, I've uncovered their uncanny
plot and I've reduced their data to one tiny, reddish dot. The
problem is, in two dimensions, it's difficult to know if the frogs
who sacrifice themselves to science suffer. Go and fondle your
minutia. Take long walks on the beach. If the skeleton's too
fragile, toss it out and make your peace with loneliness. The
rings of Saturn cautiously enfold us in more lucid everafters.
So let's not be so bold as to cite them as a "source." These books
are boring. Can't you see? The joy of reading's overrated. Watch
the DVD a bit more closely and you'll find it's an immaculate
conception. But microscopic proto-humans don't come with
instructions and it's tragic how the real questions are doomed
to pass us by, the weakest and the strongest locking horns. We
couldn't find an organ donor willing to accommodate our whims.
Keep that champagne on ice. I'll go inform her next-of-kin.

Up in the Lonely Heavens
Hieroglyphic Fever Dreams
Lament the Fate of a Grey Lock Plucked from
the Head
of a
Long-Dead Queen

Grunting "Out, out, Jezebel!"
        Caught eavesdropping mid-nap
through wounded ears god's tiny creatures hear us lying
pap to pap. I whisper things the underwater currents
would congeal to know. You pin your heart straight to
your chest and let it flutter there, just so. "Drown my
lungs in lakes," I thunder. Your angry gawks and glugs
brim the crater sweet as sainthood.

    Drowned in Lake Wastwater, confused, already
half unhypnotized we go to peel away the kiss, our
Ariels now little mermaids refusing morphine drips.

    Atop her cake the maid revolves. Her mood, carved
into melting ice, floods the *via lactea* with less than
perfect penmanship. Woven in between the lines is
night and night and all its bats. Whiny spheres caught
in their spinning. Orphaned hands and shriveled lips
inscribing one last prohibition:

    Don't go curl up in the lap of a bridesmaid
strewing comets in her wake like highway trash.

Was That Your Kid Caught Photo-Flirting on a Hallmark Holiday?

Excuse my French but, fuck it, angel, I've got something to say. *Si le prince charmant me cherche, il sait où me trouver.* Beneath an avalanche of decimals, deep-frozen in the stream of culture circulating. So, like, I had this dream. My inner Liberace was playing tribal drums with a dozen long-stemmed roses. An assemblage of warm-and-fuzzies stormed the stage and you were juggling raw pearls like fingerling potatoes. But the orthography was so unfailingly chaotic that I could barely speak about ephemera and architraves. Our walk along the beach was not so scenic, gorgeous, but don't think I didn't stare: *L'angoisse, minuit, miroirs.* You were sitting at your desk deleting, cutting, pasting, good-for-nothing flesh of flesh you tiny heartbreaker. That was the sound of *frozen* dreams, dimensionless, proverbial, and terrifying come let's nevermore be lonely thawing in the noonday sun.

Watching War Heroes Wade Through Rivers
of Forgetfulness

A purple heart. Are you afraid? The life is leaking from
our planet. They are useless stimuli, these gaudy hunks of granite.
You could let them rot for several skewed millennia and still
they wouldn't spark dead souls to life or wrest new music from
the well where Valkyries have sunk the last crude vestige of the
Rhine. They have rejected love. Now they just wait and watch
while grey creeps up their gleaming braids to burrow through
their brains. I fear the music's wet and yet the tree of life gives
shade to every parasite that gluts these oriental petals. I don't
mean to pry but I do wonder why the annals have described
your flights of silk as only semi-precious stones. I'm haunted
by the sound your purple heart makes as it shines beneath your
shifters. Lady luck! I am now tangled in your stare but, as my
mother always said, "Whatever. . . ." Would you dare defy the
letter of that logos? The old Greeks didn't groan about such
dross. They had real problems—like the East Wind as it moaned
its way toward them from Persia making doe eyes at truth. I
don't mean to pry but, it seems, despite myself, I have unearthed
another riddle from beneath your mottled glare. Love sneezes his
approval. Never mind, he's just a child whom the reader might
imagine in a green cap making light of mawkish fantasies in
which we all delight.

While Phonies Sit Enthroned Applauding Each Epiphany

Spoil the child! Let his dainty quandaries feast on more than history and science! Let his addled genius soar into a ragged scrim of lilies painted on a sky so monstrously distended the florists shake their fists before they duck and run for cover. But a stream of expletives pursues them underground like some melancholy nymph whose human lover left her for a Polish polyglot he met in Montparnasse. Watch nature type her codes along stems of green carnations while an absent-minded dawn chews on the fingers of a glove nearly withered from the heat of human bodies rubbed together. Let him sink into his psalms and run his trembling thumb across the vestibule of some old diamond-monger's arabesqued infinity—beware the silent masterpiece! A cognoscenti's call to prayer, like an adventurer at sunrise, will tip the golden bowl beyond the white dwarf's calculations. Accidents, if swallowed whole, will not embalm like butterflies inside the *musée mechanique*. This is the forest primeval, Parisians—let his infinities streak beyond your back-lit boulevards. His moods will soon out-thrill the moonless quattrocento.

Turner's skies, those far-fetched blues!

Who Jinxed This Cloud of Dust into a Blanched Diminuendo?

Lamentation shrouds a distant shore, the finely-woven sorrow of an ancient race. Tomorrow and tomorrow and tomorrow we will wash our hands in silk, we will mix our wine with blood. You thought the truth would set you free? Go detoxify, my love. It's time our hero falls into a deeper sleep. Swarms have gathered and our knives are ready to festoon the corners of this fertile crescent with a new millennium's design (a kind of pop-up prehistoric). Smile pretty, pretty. Time creeps at its petty pace, a secret history of days unraveling their endings. Chin up, soldier, if you're brave enough to formally surrender when that end comes you'll be fine. Let them put the world to sleep. One child at a time.

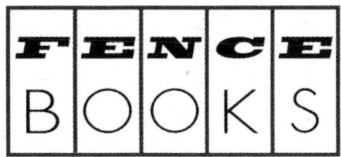

Fence Books is an extension of *Fence*, a biannual journal of poetry, fiction, art, and criticism that has a mission to redefine the terms of accessibility by publishing challenging writing distinguished by idiosyncrasy and intelligence rather than by allegiance with camps, schools, or cliques. It is part of our press's mission to support writers who might otherwise have difficulty being recognized because their work doesn't answer to either the mainstream or to recognizable modes of experimentation.

The Motherwell Prize is an annual series that offers publication of a first or second book of poems by a woman, as well as a one thousand dollar cash prize.

Our second prize series is the Fence Modern Poets Series. This contest is open to poets of any gender and at any stage of career, and offers a one thousand dollar cash prize in addition to book publication.

For more information about either prize, visit www.fenceportal.org, or send an SASE to: Fence Books/[Name of Prize], New Library 320, University at Albany, 1400 Washington Avenue, Albany, NY, 12222.

For more about *Fence*, visit www.fenceportal.org.

Fence Books

THE MOTHERWELL PRIZE

Aim Straight at the Fountain and Press Vaporize Elizabeth Marie Young
Unspoiled Air Kaisa Ullsvik Miller

THE ALBERTA PRIZE

The Cow Ariana Reines
Practice, Restraint Laura Sims
A Magic Book Sasha Steensen
Sky Girl Rosemary Griggs
The Real Moon of Poetry and Other Poems Tina Brown Celona
Zirconia Chelsey Minnis

FENCE MODERN POETS SERIES

Star in the Eye James Shea
Structure of the Embryonic Rat Brain Christopher Janke
The Stupefying Flashbulbs Daniel Brenner
Povel Geraldine Kim
The Opening Question Prageeta Sharma
Apprehend Elizabeth Robinson
The Red Bird Joyelle McSweeney

NATIONAL POETRY SERIES

Collapsible Poetics Theater Rodrigo Toscano

ANTHOLOGIES & CRITICAL WORKS

*Not for Mothers Only: Contemporary Poets on Child-Getting
    & Child-Rearing*   Catherine Wagner & Rebecca Wolff, editors

A Best of Fence: *The First Nine Years,* Volumes 1 & 2
                    Rebecca Wolff and *Fence* Editors, editors

POETRY

Stranger	Laura Sims
The Method	Sasha Steensen
The Orphan & Its Relations	Elizabeth Robinson
Site Acquisition	Brian Young
Rogue Hemlocks	Carl Martin
19 Names for Our Band	Jibade-Khalil Huffman
Infamous Landscapes	Prageeta Sharma
Bad Bad	Chelsey Minnis
Snip Snip!	Tina Brown Celona
Yes, Master	Michael Earl Craig
Swallows	Martin Corless-Smith
Folding Ruler Star	Aaron Kunin
The Commandrine & Other Poems	Joyelle McSweeney
Macular Hole	Catherine Wagner
Nota	Martin Corless-Smith
Father of Noise	Anthony McCann
Can You Relax in My House	Michael Earl Craig
Miss America	Catherine Wagner

FICTION

Flet: A Novel	Joyelle McSweeney
The Mandarin	Aaron Kunin